Writing,
Speaking,
Listening

Time-saving books that teach specific skills to busy people, focusing on what really matters; the things that make a difference – the *essentials*.

Other books in the series include:

Writing Business E-mails

Making the Most of Your Time

Coaching People

Leading Teams

Making Meetings Work

The 80/20 Management Rule

Solving Problems

Delegating

Expand Your Vocabulary

Preparing a Marketing Plan

Speaking in Public

Making Great Presentations

Writing Good Reports

Writing Great Copy

Writing,
Speaking,
Listening

Helen Wilkie

ESSENTIALS

Published in 2001 by
How To Books Ltd, 3 Newtec Place,
Magdalen Road, Oxford OX4 1RE, United Kingdom
Tel: (01865) 793806   Fax: (01865) 248780
e-mail: info@howtobooks.co.uk
www.howtobooks.co.uk

British Library Cataloguing in Publication Data.
A catalogue record for this book is available from
the British Library.

Edited by Diana Brueton
Cover design by Shireen Nathoo Design
Produced for How To Books by Deer Park Productions
Typeset by PDQ Typesetting, Newcastle-under-Lyme, Staffordshire
Printed and bound in Great Britain by Bell & Bain Ltd., Glasgow

NOTE: The material contained in this book is set out in good faith for
general guidance and no liability can be accepted for loss or expense
incurred as a result of relying in particular circumstances on
statements made in the book. Laws and regulations are complex
and liable to change, and readers should check the current position
with the relevant authorities before making personal arrangements.

ESSENTIALS *is an imprint of*
How To Books

Contents

Preface

Despite the ongoing explosion in communication technology, we often still miss the mark when it comes to communicating face-to-face or in writing. I believe the main reason for this is that we confuse information and communication, which are not the same thing at all.

While information can be a one-way flow, there is no such thing as one-way communication. For every message sent out, whether spoken or written, someone somewhere must receive and understand it – or there is no communication.

Keep this principle in mind as you work through this book.

This book provides tips and techniques for effectively conveying your message in writing. You can easily incorporate these ideas into your writing immediately, whether it be in letters, memos, reports or even e-mail messages.

After providing valuable techniques for spoken presentations, the book then goes on to look at the other side of oral communication: listening. Listening is undoubtedly the most underrated communication skill of all, and it deserves much more attention than we give to it.

The book is designed to help you assimilate the information quickly and easily. I hope you will also enjoy the process.

Helen Wilkie

1 Write for Your Audience

You might write the same message in many different ways, depending on who will be reading it.

In this chapter, three things that really matter:
~ Use language your reader will understand
~ What does this particular reader need to know?
~ Adopt a pleasant tone

The objective of business writing is to communicate a message. This is always the case, even when we are writing a report or memo 'just for the file'. Many letters, memos and reports fail in this objective because they are written for the writer, not the reader.

Unlike other written materials – such as novels, plays or poetry – business correspondence must clearly convey its message to the reader, preferably on first reading. People are busy in today's business world and they don't have time to study letters, looking for obscure meaning. Let this be your warning and your guideline: if they have to read it twice, they probably won't.

Before beginning to write, ask yourself the question, 'Who is my reader for this particular letter?' Visualize and write for that person and you will have a good chance of getting your message across.

Is this you?

• I explained all this in my letter – why didn't he understand? • I always feel I have to explain all the details. • I can't believe she reacted so badly to my memo – I never meant to imply she was at fault.

Use language your reader will understand

Suppose you are a doctor performing specialized tests on patients. At the end of each procedure you must send a written report on the tests to the patient, with a copy to the family doctor. Would you send the same report to both? Without stopping to think about it, many of us would. Yet one of these readers is familiar with medical terminology, while the other may be terrified by it. In business correspondence, this happens all the time.*

Jargon is a set of words, phrases or initials whose meaning is automatically known to people within a specific group. This may be a profession, an industry, a company, a political or religious association or any other group. Because of the common interests of the individual members, they develop a kind of shorthand which they all understand. Often, jargon is the most effective way of communicating with the group.

A problem arises, however, when we step outside the group. Too often we forget that outsiders don't understand our special inside language.

Here are a few examples of jargon from various industries and professions. How many

* *One of the main barriers to communication in business correspondence is the inappropriate use of jargon.*

do you understand?

(a) 70lb duplex coated

(b) style of cause

(c) laparoscopic procedure

(d) full bleed

(e) upper deck masking

(f) GAAP.

Answers:

(a) Printers know this is a type of paper.

(b) In the legal profession, court documents might begin with the words, 'In the case of Smith vs Jones'. That's the style of cause.

(c) Your surgeon might use special probing instruments in conjunction with a computer to look around your innards and perhaps remove tissue. That's a laparoscopic procedure.

(d) In printing, when the ink goes right to the edge of the paper, it's called full bleed.

(e) In a stadium or other large venue, if the crowd is 30,000 and there are 40,000 seats, they might cover – or mask – the extra 10,000 on the upper level.

(f) Generally Accepted Accounting Principles.

You probably didn't know all of these terms – and there's no reason why you should, because they are other people's jargon. So next time you use a term specific to your group, ask yourself if this particular reader can reasonably be expected to understand. If not, find a way to say it in plain language.*

What does this particular reader need to know?

Why are you writing this letter to this particular person? ('Because my boss told me to write it' doesn't count!) What you need to focus on is the message your letter should convey. Then, make every word, every sentence and every paragraph work towards that specific goal.

Let's say your manager has asked you to

* *Write to express, not to impress.*

research a possible new market and make a recommendation on whether or not the company should try to penetrate it. Too often, such a report begins something like this:

> 'You asked me to investigate the growing demand for superwidgets, who is buying them, possible manufacturers of the various types of the product...blah, blah, blah...'

Why are you saying all this? You are writing to the person who asked you to take on the task, so he or she already knows! A reader's attention is at its highest in the first couple of sentences, so don't waste the opportunity to engage attention. Here's a better approach:

> 'As a result of my investigation of the growing demand for superwidgets, I strongly recommend we enter this market as soon as possible.'

Before starting to write, think of the questions your reader might ask about your subject. The answers can form the basis for the written piece. Here are just a few examples.

To answer this possible question:	*You might write:*
~ When will the new version of the software be available?	~ We are pleased to announce that Version 3 of our best-selling ACME software will be shipped to customers on February 15.
~ Why are we so short of cash?	~ A shortage of skilled staff in the accounting department has meant that invoices have been sent out 30 days late. This means that incoming payments are delayed, while we still must meet our outgoing payment obligations. As a result, our cash reserves are lower than normal.
~ Who is this person and why is she writing to me?	~ As a qualified graphic layout artist with ten years of experience, I would like an opportunity to discuss with you the possibility of working with your firm.

A well known company specializing in the manufacture of toys for very young children requires its product development people to spend time crawling around on all-fours. Why? When they are on their hands and knees, their eyes are at the same level as the eye level of the little people for whom they are creating a product. In other words, if they see the product from the point of view of the user, it will have a better chance of success.

Similarly, if you can, just for a moment, get into your reader's mind and find out what that person needs to know, you can write a letter that conveys appropriate information, couched in appropriate language.*

Adopt a pleasant tone

* If you drown your readers in detail, it is quite likely that their eyes will glaze over and they will completely miss your message. Tell them only what they need to know.

When we think of tone, we usually think of a sound, such as the human voice. We know when someone is annoyed by the tone of voice they use in speaking. We know if they are being polite, or sarcastic, or amused. In writing, tone is just as important, but because the other person can't hear the sound of the words, those words have to speak clearly on the printed page – or the computer screen.

Perhaps you have heard the expression, 'You catch more bears with honey than you do with vinegar.' Did you ever stop to think you may be dripping vinegar all over your business letters without ever realizing it? Many of the letters we send to one another in business are much less pleasant than we imagine, and many create a tone we never intended.

The following two groups of words illustrate what I mean:

Vinegar

blame, fault, careless, failure, inferior, negligence, penalty, complaint

Honey

please, thank you, appreciate, understand, agree, excellent, service, value

Try reading the words aloud and think about how you would use them in speech, and then in writing.

When we use the vinegar words, we automatically set up a negative environment in the reader's mind, and the response is likely to be negative. The opposite is true when we use honey words.

If I said to you, 'Robert did not attend the meeting last week,' what would you think? You would probably take it at face value, that Robert wasn't at the meeting. However, if I said instead, 'Robert failed to attend the meeting last week,' wouldn't that change your perspective? That suggests that he should have been there, and the fact that he wasn't implies a failure of some kind. How often do we use words such as 'failure' without ever intending to be judgmental? But being judgmental is the result.*

Here is a paragraph positively dripping with vinegar.

> 'Having just received your complaint with regard to our new software programme, I must say I completely fail to understand why you should be confused. We enclosed three instructional manuals with the programme, all of which have been compiled by technically competent

* *People are more likely to do or think as you want them to if you allow them to do so with their egos intact.*

personnel and which should be readily understood by anyone with a basic education. We have received no other complaints, and so I must conclude we are not at fault and cannot agree to your demand for a refund.'

Try rewriting it yourself before reading my rewritten version below.

'I am sorry you had a problem with the manuals for our new software. Although we have done our best to make our manuals user friendly, complex software such as this can still be confusing. So that you won't miss out on the benefits of the great new product, I would like to speak to you by phone and try to clear up your questions. Please call me any time this week, and if this is acceptable to you we can talk through the process. I very much want to be of assistance to you and look forward to your call.'

Which one would be more likely to retain a valuable client?

Summary points

★   When tempted to use jargon, ask yourself if this particular reader can be reasonably expected to understand. If not, change it to plain English.

★   Visualize your reader and think about his or her information needs. Consider what questions that person might ask about your subject, and answer them.

★   Create a positive environment in your reader's mind through the positive words you choose. Even a negative message will be better received if it is expressed in language that respects the reader's dignity.

2 Choose the Right Words and the Right Structure

To write effectively in business you must be proficient in the use of the three building blocks of writing: words, sentences and paragraphs.

In this chapter, five things that really matter:
~ Use the right word in the right place
~ Simple words highlight your message
~ Cut out the fluff
~ The sentence is the driver of the message
~ The paragraph: a unit of thought

If sitting down to write a business letter or memo leaves you feeling overwhelmed, remember it's like any other task – easier when broken down into manageable chunks.

There are three steps to developing your writing competency.

First, become familiar with basic grammar. English grammar is logical and if your grammar or syntax are incorrect you may well be saying something other than what you intend. Consider the following examples:

> 'I won almost a million pounds in the lottery.'

> 'I almost won a million pounds in the lottery.'

What a different syntax makes! It's not the purpose of this book to teach you grammar, but there are many excellent books available. There are also many places on the Internet where you can find this information, so there is no shortage of resources.

Second, work on techniques to make your writing not only grammatically correct, but also clear, concise and interesting.

Third, practice.

Is this you?

• I often mix up words and am not sure which is the right one. • Won't people be more impressed if I use fancy words in business letters? • People always tell me my memos and letters are too long. • My sentences tend to ramble and I never feel they convey my message clearly. • How many sentences are in a paragraph?

Use the right words in the right place

English is a rich language, which is usually a good thing. However, there is one nasty little trick lying in wait for the unwary writer:

~ pairs of words that look similar and appear to have the same meanings – but they don't.

Sometimes there are just shades of difference, but at other times they mean totally different things. Business writers often confuse these words, playing havoc with meaning.

Test yourself on the following commonly confused pairs:

1. eminent/imminent
2. complement/compliment
3. apprised/appraised
4. stationery/stationary
5. flaunt/flout
6. uninterested/disinterested
7. eg/i.e.

8. currently/presently
9. council/counsel
10. ensure/insure

Here are the meanings, and some sentences to illustrate how the words are used.

1. A number of eminent persons attended the gala (*eminent* means *prominent* or *powerful*).

    The Prime Minister's speech suggests that an election call is imminent (*imminent* means *about to happen*).

2. These new curtains complement the furnishings of the room (*complement* means *go together with*).

    Thank you for your gracious compliment (a *compliment* is a positive *comment*).

3. As a technology consultant, you should keep your clients apprised of the latest equipment (*apprised* means *informed*).

    I must have my jewellery appraised for insurance purposes (*appraised* means *valued*).

4. We must order more stationery (*stationery*

means *paper, envelopes, etc.*).

The child ran out from behind a stationary vehicle (*stationary* means *not moving*).

5. If you've got it, flaunt it! (*flaunt* means *show off*).

   A rebel is someone who flouts authority. (*flout* means *go against*).

6. I am completely uninterested in this. (*uninterested* means *doesn't care*). The judge in a court case must be a disinterested party (*disinterested* means *impartial*).

7. I love Italian food, eg pasta primavera (eg means *for example*). The terms are set out in the contract we signed, i.e. the Purchase and Sale Agreement (*i.e.* means *that is*).

8. My father is currently president of the golf club (*currently* means *at present*).

   I'm sorry to keep you waiting, but I will be with you presently (*presently* means *soon*).

9. The municipal council met to discuss the new by-law (a *council* is a *committee*).

    I always appreciate your wise counsel (*counsel* means *advice*; it can also be used as a verb meaning to *give advice* or it can also be the person giving the advice as in *legal counsel*).

10. Please ensure that the package goes out in tonight's mail (*ensure* means *make sure*).

    You should insure your new house against fire and theft (*insure* means *to protect* and should only be used in the sense of insurance policies).

If you use these (or other) words incorrectly in your business writing, it does terrible things to your credibility. Fortunately, there is a simple tool to correct the problem: a dictionary. Most people have a dictionary by their desks, but many of them would free a colony of moths if they were taken off the shelf because they are rarely used.*

* *Keep a dictionary near you, and use it when you are in doubt about either spelling or meaning.*

By the way, your computer's 'spellcheck' won't help you here. It will tell you when you have made up a word that doesn't exist, but it won't tell you when you have used *imminent* when you meant *eminent*.

Simple words highlight your message

Professionals, in particular, seem to have a problem with the idea of using simple words, because they're afraid people will think they are not well-educated. But they won't. If you use simple words, people won't notice them at all because they will be too busy getting the message. That's called communication, and it's the object of the exercise!

Examples

Here are some examples of simple words you can substitute for complex ones.

Locate/find

Why do business letters insist on locating files – or people – when normal conversation would just find them?

Furnish/provide

Imagine you come from another country and English is not your first language. How confused you would be seeing a word you associate with tables and chairs in the context of information movement!

Terminate/finish

If you are in the legal profession you may have to use *terminate* in contracts and other legal documents. But don't carry it over to ordinary correspondence – it's much better to use the simpler word.

Optimum/best

Some simple words tend to fall into disuse because people think the fancier version sounds more important. You may be surprised to know that not everyone knows what *optimum* means. But everyone understands *best*.

Forward/send

Forward is properly used to say something is sent from one person to another and then on to another. The first person in the chain, however, doesn't forward but merely sends.

Concept/idea

The advertising industry has raised the word *concept* to special status. When the client has an idea, it's just an idea. But the agency's idea becomes The Concept. A group of people sitting round a table throwing ideas around is usually said to be brainstorming. But when the ad agency people do it, it's called conceptualization – and it's very expensive!

What simpler versions of the following words could you use?

utilize, parameters, paradigm, commencement, expedite, cognizant, diminutive, iteration

This doesn't mean that you must never use a more complex word, but several in one sentence make for heavy reading. This automatically makes them a barrier to communication.*

* So when there is a choice – and there almost always is – lean towards the simple word.

Cut out the fluff

Many a two-page letter could be reduced to one page if we would just stop saying things like *in the majority of instances* when we mean *usually*.

Why do we say *as you may or may not know*? If you may know, then obviously you may not know. That's what *may* means. If you think they probably know, say *as you may know*. If you think they don't, say *as you may not know*, but you don't need the whole thing.

Where did *at this point in time* come from? It seems to be some sort of attempt to bring cosmic significance to something quite ordinary! What's wrong with *at present*, or *now*?

People often use wordy phrases such as *of a confidential nature* instead of a perfectly good, serviceable adjective like *confidential*. The same applies to *historical*, *legal*, *private* and many others.

When you can use a single word instead of a phrase, without losing any meaning, choose the word.

How would you replace these often-used

'fluffy' phrases?

~ proceeding in a westerly direction
~ on a daily basis
~ 27 years of age
~ red in colour.

Another common form of fluff is the phrase containing redundant words.

One example is *new breakthrough* – have you ever heard of an old breakthrough? The word *breakthrough* stands on its own, and its meaning is clear.

Here's another: *This young man has a great future ahead of him*. Where else would his future be but ahead?

The other side of that is *past history*. History is, by definition, past – you don't need to define it again.

And what about *the honest truth*? Is there another kind?

We often write *very unique*. *Unique* is a word we have stolen from the French language – the least we can do is use it correctly. It doesn't mean *unusual*. It means there is only one. So something cannot be very unique, somewhat unique, rather unique or even quite unique. It might be very unusual – but it's either unique or it's not.

And since it's in the nature of an emergency to take us by surprise, why do we say *unexpected emergency*?

Here are a few more to eliminate from your writing. What could you say instead?

~ foreign import
~ absolutely perfect
~ necessary requisite
~ permission and approval
~ due and payable
~ the resulting consequence
~ 10 a.m. in the morning.

Think twice next time you use any of these.*

The sentence is the driver of the message

At the very least, your sentences should be grammatically correct. If this is an area of weakness for you, invest in one of the many books available on the subject. Study the text, and then keep it close to your desk as a

* When editing what you have written, look for instances where you have said the same thing twice, and take out the fluff.

reference for those times when you have a question.

As drivers of effective business writing, however, your sentences must be more than just grammatically correct – they must be powerful. They must express your message clearly, concisely and with no room for misunderstanding.*

To build such a sentence, you need only follow the four guidelines described below.

1. For the most part, write in the active voice. The voice has to do with whether the subject of the sentence is the person or thing taking the action, or the person or thing being written about. Let's look at what that means in the following sentences.

    'The chairman made a great speech.' In this example the chairman is the subject of the sentence because he is taking the action of making a speech. This is called the **active voice**.

    'A great speech was made by the chairman.' In this case the subject being

*   Write grammatically correct and well crafted sentences, and you will be halfway to an effective written piece.

written about is the speech, and we call this construction the **passive voice**. The **passive voice** comes in two forms: the **regular passive**, as in the above example, and the **divine passive**. In the latter form, the person doing the action is not mentioned at all. For example, 'A serious mistake has been made.'

With the divine passive nobody does things – they just mysteriously happen. Who made this serious mistake? We don't know. The attraction of this form, of course, is that we can make statements without taking responsibility for them. If you say, for example, 'You will be contacted when your order is ready', that gives your reader no assurance that you will do the contacting. A little of this goes a long way, as repeated use tends to create the feeling that things are not as they appear. It also makes for tedious reading.

2. Make your verbs the powerful tools they should be. For example, 'I have written three books' carries more power than 'I

am the writer of three books.' In the second the verb 'am' must be linked to something because it tells us nothing by itself. When you write a sentence like this, ask yourself the question, 'If we are in agreement, what do we do?' The answer is, 'We agree.'

3. Use specific words rather than those that leave interpretation up to the reader. Too many letters contain, for example, words and phrases such as *report*, *document*, *handle*, *fix*, *deal with*. Each one can be understood in different ways, depending on context. It's not your reader's job to figure out what you mean, but yours to make it clear. Be specific.

4. Don't ramble. Convoluted sentences hide meaning. Look at this example:

    'The manager, thinking the meeting was at 10 a.m., as was his original understanding based on the first notice, arrived as usual at 9.30 a.m., very surprised and none too pleased to find it already in progress, under the direction of his deputy, at 9.15 a.m.'

A sentence like this needs to be broken into more than one sentence, and then streamlined even more:

'Based on the first notice, the manager thought the meeting would begin at 10 a.m., and he arrived at 9.30 a.m. To his surprise and displeasure, the meeting had begun at 9.15 a.m. under the direction of his deputy.'

The paragraph: a unit of thought

People often ask me how many sentences are in a paragraph. Well, it's not as simple as that. There is no set number of sentences in a paragraph, and that's not the important thing anyway. What counts is the way you put your sentences together. Think of a paragraph as a unit of thought: one thought, one paragraph. Here's a good way to build a powerful paragraph.

~ The key sentence sets the scene, telling the reader what the paragraph is about.

~ The next two or three sentences provide support for the key sentence statement.

~ Finally, the concluding sentence brings the meaning full circle and emphasises the key.

The following paragraphs illustrates this construction:

> 'I am a creature of impulse. Just yesterday I decided to visit Spain for a week. Within two hours I had booked my flight, arranged a hotel and bought a new swimsuit. I spent all last night dreaming of the warm Spanish sun and the sound of castanets. Still, tomorrow I might just as well cancel the whole thing and stay at home.
>
> 'Most people take longer to plan, and I sometimes think I would do better to copy them. But I like to do things on the spur of the moment.'

Note, the paragraph break comes at a point where another aspect is brought in: other people's habits in comparison to the writer's.*

* A paragraph is a unit of thought: one thought, one paragraph.

Summary points

★   If you are not sure which of a pair of words to use, check your dictionary.

★   Don't burden your reader with complicated words and expressions when simple words would convey your message more clearly. Write to express, not impress.

★   Streamline your sentences by removing extra words and phrases that say the same thing twice. When you can reduce your word count without taking away any of the meaning, do so.

★   Study grammar until it becomes second nature. Then craft your sentences in the active voice, using specific words and action verbs. Don't ramble.

★   When you introduce a new topic, or a new aspect of the same topic, take a new paragraph. Set the scene, give details and reiterate your key statement.

3 To Present Effectively You Need a Strategy

If you don't know where you are going, how will you know when you are there? An effective presentation requires a roadmap.

In this chapter, five things that really matter:
~ Set your objective
~ Know your audience
~ Consider your pre-presentation tactics
~ Plan your approach
~ Open and close with a bang

There was a time, not so long ago, when only managers and executives made business presentations. Today, that has changed. People at all levels are expected to be able to present their ideas and plans competently and enthusiastically to various audiences both within the organization and outside. Thus, to have career success today it's not enough just to do your job well, but you must be *seen* to do it well. One way of raising your visibility is to make effective presentations.

Whether you are actually selling a product or service, or just your ideas and ability, every time you stand up to make a presentation you are selling – and those who do it well are those who succeed. Whether it's fair or not, it's a fact that those who present well are perceived as doing everything well.*

Is this you?

• I find myself rambling all around the subject when I present. • What went over well with management didn't fly with the sales force. • Sometimes I am surprised by unexpected opposition to my ideas. • I'm afraid to miss out something important, so I put in everything and my presentations are too long. • I don't know how to begin and my endings are an anti-climax.

* *Every presentation is an opportunity to advance your career.*

Set your objective

Everyone in the room comes to your

presentation with his or her own expectations. You have no control over other people's expectations, but you can and must be very clear about your own. If you don't know what you want to achieve, you can't do an effective job of planning your presentation.

Ask yourself why you are giving the presentation. What is your purpose? What do you want your audience to know, to understand, to feel, to do at the end of it? This question is so important that I suggest you begin the planning process by writing on a piece of paper the following words:

At the end of this presentation, I want...

Then complete the statement as specifically as possible, eg at the end of this presentation, I want the board to approve my plan to introduce a new benefits programme by the first quarter of next year. Notice, this is not only specific, but measurable. The board will either approve the plan or not; I will have achieved my objective or not.

Although it's not always possible to have such a measurable objective, do be as specific as possible. An appropriate objective will stop you from rambling.*

One of the most challenging presentation situations is the monthly departmental report. If you simply stand up and recite financial information – we sold so much, it cost so much, our profit was so much – your audience will almost certainly switch off mentally before you go very far. But what is the alternative? Well, when setting your objective, continue to go deeper into the reasons for the presentation. Here is a sample of the type of questioning you might do.

~ **Statement**: At the end of this presentation I want the management group to know our financial results for the month.

~ **Question**: Why?

~ **Statement**: Because they need to know how we have done.

~ **Question**: Why?

~ **Statement**: So that they will know why we couldn't meet the target figures.

~ **Question**: Why?

* *You can't control your audience's expectations, so concentrate on your own.*

~ **Statement**: So that we can make adjustments for the next quarter.

~ **Question**: What adjustments?

~ **Statement**: Well, if we get the one more salesperson I have been asking for we can meet the sales target. Otherwise, we need to lower the sales objective.

~ **Question**: So ... at the end of this presentation, what do I want?

~ **Statement**: At the end of this presentation, I want the management group to understand why our results were below projections and what we should do to correct this in the next quarter.

Do you see how the last version of the objective will make for a more effective, meaningful presentation? If you have this objective in front of you as you plan, you can include suggestions that will help lead your audience where you want them to go. So don't just settle for a boring recital of facts – use your presentation to help you get what you want.

Know your audience

Who your audience is should govern how you present your material, so one of your first tasks will be to analyze the group to whom you will be presenting.*

Here are some questions to ask yourself.

~ Are they part of my organization or outsiders? Do they have technical knowledge of my topic or not? The answers to these questions will tell you whether you can 'speak in tongues' or whether you must omit all forms of jargon; whether you should go into technical details, or give them just the surface information.

~ Do they know me? Are we on friendly terms? These answers can help determine your overall approach to the group.

~ Are they likely to be hostile? If you are introducing a new programme, you need to know if it is not likely to be well received. Do your homework to find out where they stand – and tailor your

* The right presentation to the wrong people is the wrong presentation.

programme to win them over.

~ Have they heard it all before? A bored audience makes for an ineffective presentation. Perhaps you need to come up with new slants, new emphasis. Should you introduce some controversy? Personal research can bring out little known facts to start people thinking of things differently. Can you raise their level of interest by involving them in some way in your presentation, rather than just talking to them?

~ How many will be there? Addressing 500 people in an auditorium is quite different from a small group meeting in a conference room.

~ Are they my seniors, juniors or peers? This can affect what you say, as well as how you say it.

Consider your pre-presentation tactics

Based on your knowledge of the audience, there are some things you can do in advance to help your presentation meet its objective.

If you think your new programme will be a hard sell, for example, it helps to know you have at least some allies in the room. You might approach some you already know are sympathetic to your cause and enlist their support. You might even arrange a way in which you can call upon one person during the presentation to 'confirm' a point that will help you.

At the same time, it is good to know who will be the strongest voices against you, and prepare to back up your viewpoints.

If your audience is made up of financial or systems people, focus on logic to make your points. Such individuals usually prefer lots of back-up information and detail. Even if you don't use all of it in the presentation, be prepared to offer it in response to questions. If your audience is a group of salespeople, on the other hand, emotional appeals can work well. Salespeople are usually competitive and will often respond well to motivational language.

If gaining credibility with your audience is

a consideration, you might send a business biography or other evidence of your credentials before the meeting or work with the person who will introduce you to let the audience see why you are the right person to give the presentation.*

Plan your approach

Poor arrangement of content is one of the most common reasons for a failed presentation. Presenters are often tempted to tell the audience everything they know about the subject, and there are two problems with this. First, too much information will overwhelm listeners and they will simply switch off. Second, so much material is extremely difficult to organize, so it can easily overwhelm the presenter too!

Decide what information to include in your talk, what to put in the form of handouts and what to omit altogether. It helps to refer to your written objective during this process. For each segment of information, ask yourself if this will move you towards your objective. If

* *Doing your homework paves the way for success in your presentation.*

not, take it out.

Decide what format will best suit the information.*

Here are some sample formats that are readily adaptable to many situations.

Problem/solution

This format is the presenter's friend! Women's magazines sometimes feature 'makeovers' showing how the subjects improved their appearance by changing hairstyle, makeup, clothing, etc. The 'before' photograph shows the person in the least attractive light, while the 'after' shot takes all possible advantage of lighting, positioning and professional expertise to emphasize the effects of the changes. You can use this ploy in your presentation. Identify a problem, then describe it in terms that point out the breadth and depth of the difficulty. Now dazzle them with your solution!

Goal/roadmap

This is effective only if you identify a goal

* A logical format makes it easier for you to present and easier for the audience to understand.

which the audience will accept. Larger market share, leadership of an industry, or a cure for a deadly disease are goals that lend themselves to this formula. Set out the goal, and then focus on 'how we can get there from here'.

Objections/answers

If you want to sell an idea to an audience you know well, this can be effective. Simply think of all the objections they are likely to raise, and counter them methodically throughout your presentation. Answer all their objections in advance, and they have nothing left to fight your proposals, and your presentation has a good chance of success.

Topical

If you have a number of unrelated topics, joined only by means of your presentation, this is the format to use. The key to making it a coherent presentation, however, is to create smooth transitions from one topic to the next. It is also helpful if you can weave a common thread through all the topics.

Chronological

This is probably the least interesting format, but may be suitable when you must give some history to illustrate a situation.

Open and close with a bang

The legal profession gives us a principle called the Law of Primacy and Recency. Never heard of it? All it means is that people remember best what they heard first and what they heard last. Andrew Lloyd Webber knows all about this principle, and uses it to great effect. Follow the crowd milling out of the theatre after one of his shows, and what music will they be humming? That's right – the big closing number, which is often a reprise of the big opening number! How can you use this in your presentations?

Openings

In the first moments of your presentation you must grab your audience's attention. No matter whether you are addressing the whole company in an auditorium, the board of directors in the boardroom or your department at the weekly sales meeting, you must capture their attention and give them a reason to listen to you. Contrary to popular belief among presenters, there is no such thing as a captive audience. They may be there in the seats, but they can leave mentally any time they wish. Don't give them a reason.

As soon as you stand up, hit them with a statement or question that makes them sit up and take notice. For example, a presentation on the need to back up computerized data regularly might start with:

> 'Last week all activity in this Division ground to a halt because a virus invaded the hard drive and all the data was lost.'

That should get their attention, and you can go into more or less detail depending on your audience and the information available. The more dramatic the impact, the better. Now you can go on to talk about how to prevent such a disaster by backing up data.

I suggest you write out the first couple of minutes of your speech. Then, translate it from the written word (eg cannot, will not, there is) to the spoken form (eg can't, won't, there's), which makes it sound more natural. Finally, memorize your opening. That will allow you to make eye contact with your audience as you begin, the first step in creating rapport.

Close with a bang

Whatever you want your audience to take from your presentation should be addressed in your close. Take your cue from the classic sales advice and ask for the order: 'Bearing in mind the potential gains from this exciting initiative, I ask for your approval today.'

Reviewing the major points of your presentation can bring it to a successful close. Remember, though, that this should be a summary, not a repetition of the details.*

A great quote can also serve to focus your audience's attention. There are many collections of quotes available in print and on the Internet, and you can almost always find one that exactly suits your purpose.

As with the opening, write down, translate and memorize the close. You can then

* *Tell them what you're going to tell them, tell them, then tell them what you told them.*

practise and deliver a close that would make Andrew Lloyd Webber proud!

Summary points

★ Be clear in your mind what you want out of the presentation, and design your content to move towards that objective. Without a specific objective, you have no measure of your success.

★ Knowing who your audience is will help you decide how to frame your information in appropriate language. The message can be affected by the number of people and your relationship to them. What works for your own department may not work for management.

★ Some research before the presentation can eliminate unpleasant surprises in the form of unexpected opposition. Line up some support in advance.

★ Choose the right amount of information for the allotted time and structure it around a format. This makes it easier on you as well as your listeners.

★   Grab their attention with your opening statement and give them a reason to continue listening to you. Use your close to direct them to the action or response you want from them.

4 Make Your Visuals Aid

They're called 'visual aids' because they are designed to aid your presentation.

In this chapter, four things that really matter:
~ Choose the form of visual aid that best suits the occasion
~ Two mistakes to avoid at all costs
~ A picture is worth many words
~ Visual aids should not double as handouts

If you ever doubt the importance of visual aids, just ask those who have to listen to presentations in the course of their jobs. Effective visuals can double the impact of your message. Some people are visual learners, taking in information predominantly by eye, while others learn more from what they hear. However, it is generally agreed that information which is presented both verbally and visually is not only more likely to be absorbed and understood, but will be remembered for a longer time. That's the rationale behind supporting your spoken presentation with slides, flipcharts, computer images or other forms of visual aid.

Too often, however, presenters underestimate the importance of this valuable tool, and their presentations suffer. They spend most of the time thinking about what they will say, and the visual aids are almost an afterthought. If this is your pattern, you do yourself a disservice. In this section, we will look at how to create visuals that will truly be an aid to your presentation.

Is this you?

• I am nervous about presentation technology – must I use it? • When I put up spreadsheets, I don't get a chance to go through them because audience members are asking me questions. • I don't know how to illustrate my talk. • The management committee members are so busy reading the handouts they don't listen to me.

Choose the form of visual aid that best suits the occasion

The range of options is growing all the time, particularly the high-tech choices. However, it's important to realize that high-tech is not always necessary, nor even the best choice. Your choice of vehicle depends on a number of factors, including the size of the audience and the room, the formality of the occasion, the level of sophistication of the material and the expectations of the audience. Here are some of the options, beginning with the simplest.

Flipcharts

This old standby still has its place, and the fact that manufacturers continue to produce new and improved easels indicates they expect it to be around for some time. Flipcharts are fairly informal, and the visibility of the content is limited by distance from the stand. So smaller meeting and training rooms are suitable venues. They are useful for making notes and drawing diagrams in the course of discussions. At least one manufacturer now makes a pad with self-adhesive sheets that can be put up on a wall without doing any damage. This allows you to post all the sheets around the room for later discussion or note-taking.

Tip: If you must make a drawing on a flipchart during your presentation, draw it lightly in pencil before the meeting. This will be invisible from any distance, and all the audience sees is you producing a brilliant illustration of your point right before their eyes. Impressive!

Whiteboards

Like flipcharts, whiteboards are useful for making notes and drawings during meetings. The drawback traditionally was that there could be only one frame of data at a time, previous information being lost when the board was wiped clean. This old favourite, however, has now been dramatically updated to an electronic version. You write or draw on it in the usual way, but instead of cleaning it off you simply transfer the information into a computer with the touch of a few buttons.

Thus, the results of the discussion can be reproduced in clean form for distribution. Some models can even be hooked up to the Internet, so that meeting participants in different locations can take an active part in the discussion and see the visuals.

Overhead transparencies

With the advent of computer presentations, many have predicted the quick demise of the lowly overhead. However, to paraphrase Mark Twain, reports of their death have been greatly exaggerated. They are quick and easy to make, in black and white or colour, and no matter where you are making your presentation, there is almost certainly an overhead projector available – with no compatibility problems. They are also easy to carry in a briefcase and to store in a three-ring binder.

35mm slides

These are generally considered one level up from overheads. However, although the effects can be polished and professional, they do have drawbacks. Since they must be processed by a photo service, it is inconvenient to make changes. You can never be sure of the effects of your colour choice until you project them, often leaving no time to make adjustments. The biggest drawback, though, is the fact that you must dim the lights to show them, and most presenters like to be able to see the audience.

Presentation software

This represents the latest advances in presentation technology to date. These programmes allow you to create remarkable graphic effects, including moving objects, zooming letters and even sound effects. The screens are easily modified, so lend themselves to customization of your presentation right up to the moment you begin. This is a great advantage if you make a similar presentation to many groups but need to change the details for each audience. Used properly, they can greatly enhance a presentation. There are, however, three potential drawbacks.

~ First, you must have a computer and projector which are not only compatible with each other, but also with the audiovisual system in the presentation room. Too many presentations fall apart or begin half an hour late while incompatibilities are corrected.

~ Second, presenters often have trouble keeping the technology on track during the presentation and it is not unusual for screens to mysteriously skip or run ahead of the programme. It's painful for an audience to watch a presenter fiddle with buttons while trying to match the visuals to the commentary.

~ Last, and worst of all, there is the potential for presenters to become carried away with the possibilities. Just because the software allows you to insert all kinds of special effects doesn't mean it is appropriate. In business presentations, less is often more. You want the audience to be paying attention to you, not watching wide-eyed while a firework display takes place in the background!

Choose your visual aid vehicle based on its appropriateness for the situation, as well as your own level of comfort in using it. If you must go high-tech and you are not familiar with the equipment, take some training first to ensure your visuals help, and don't hinder, your presentation.*

Two mistakes to avoid at all costs

Here's a common scenario among less successful business presenters. The company accountant must make a financial presentation to the Board of Directors. Since she dreads the event so much she leaves it until the last minute before she begins to prepare the presentation. At the 'eleventh hour' she finally dictates her speech and has it typed up in large letters, double spaced. If there are six people expected at the meeting, she makes six copies and then, almost as an afterthought, one extra on overhead transparencies. The pages of this last copy then become her visual aids!

* *High-tech, low-tech or no tech? It's your choice.*

1.   Pity the poor audience who must sit

through this, the presenter puts up a slide completely full of words in one or two paragraphs. Often we can't read it, but that doesn't matter because the speaker then turns around, addresses the screen and reads it for us. Then, just in case we miss a word, we can refer to our handouts – which are an exact copy – and read it ourselves! You have to ask yourself why the presentation is needed at all. A memo would have accomplished the same objective.

2. Because of the nature of her information, our comptroller makes the other classic visual aid mistake: she puts up transparencies of large, complicated financial statements. When you do that you can guarantee that at no point will the attention of all your audience members be focused exactly where you want it to be. There's simply too much for them to try to take in – and of course they are no longer listening to you. This is a control issue. It's your presentation and you need to make sure the

audience's attention is with you all the way. Don't lose them because they are wading through masses of data on your slides.*

A picture is worth many words

If the information on your screen is competing with you for audience attention, you will lose. For this reason people should be able to absorb the visual information quickly. This means as few words as possible and, where appropriate, graphic devices that convey their message instantly.

Here are some suggestions for conveying financial information as part of your presentation.

~ Comparisons between sums of money, such as this year vs last year, or actual vs budget, can be shown by **bar charts**. Sums of money are typically shown as vertical columns, while lengths of time are usually horizontal bars. Generally, avoid 3D bars, as they can be confusing. Flat ones in contrasting colours work well.

* *Masses of words or figures will not be an aid to you or your audience.*

~ The relationship of parts to a whole, such as product or service mix, jumps right off the screen when shown as a **pie chart**. You can add to the effect by 'exploding' pie charts, where individual slices seem to separate from the whole pie. Don't get carried away with special effects though – remember, the data is the important thing.

~ Trends are clear when shown as **graphs**. You can even show a number of trends on the same graph by using different coloured lines or dotted/dashed lines. Don't use too many figures, as they make your graphs too cluttered and hard to read.

~ For information that doesn't lend itself to graphic representation, use words. But instead of large blocks of text, use **word charts**. These are series of bullet points made up of phrases rather than sentences. Say just enough to highlight what you will talk about, so that people will glance at the screen and then bring their attention back to you.

~ In appropriate circumstances, **cartoons**

and other pictures can give great impact to your message.*

Do *not* use illustrations from magazines and other sources, as this is an infringement of copyright. Instead, search the Internet for what is called 'clip art', some available without charge and some for which you must pay. Used judiciously, these graphic devices can create a light moment that adds another dimension to your talk.

It is very frustrating to audience members if they can't read your slides because letters and figures are too small. (Some presenters will even draw attention to this fact by saying, 'You probably can't read this at the back', which invites the audience to wonder why the slides are there at all.) Use the space on the screen. If you are using transparencies, type up the information and print it. Now place the slide on the floor at your feet, with a light background behind it. If you can read the lettering from a standing position, it will project clearly for the audience. If you are using 35 mm slides, hold them up to a light at arm's length. If you can read it, so will your

* *A picture conveys its information instantly, freeing the audience's attention for the presenter's words.*

audience.

In creating word charts, follow the '6 x 6' guideline: no more than six words to a line, no more than six lines to a screen. If you keep roughly to this count, and fill the frame with the words, your visual aids will be comfortably read by the audience.

It is important to be able to focus your audience's attention where you want it at any time. I have found the best tool for this purpose is the laser pointer. It's small enough to fit in your hand when not in use, and its sharp, bright red presence draws everyone's eyes wherever it goes on the screen. Buy a good quality laser pointer, and make sure it always has fresh batteries.

Visual aids should not double as handouts

The ideal visual aid contains just enough information to support what you say. Handouts, on the other hand, should serve as reminders for later use, or to give complete information to supplement the presentation. If you are discussing financial information, for example, you might use charts and graphs as visuals, fill in some of the details in your speech, and hand out a complete set of financial statements. Don't make the mistake of handing these out at the beginning of your presentation, because people will spend your time perusing them. Tell them they will receive complete statements at the end, but that you want to focus on specific aspects during your speech.

When I am asked to provide a set of my slides in advance to be inserted in an audience binder, I try to decline the request. If your slides are appropriate for their purpose, they will not contain enough information to be useful handouts.*

Summary points

★   There is a growing range of options in the form of visual aids you can use. Choose one that is appropriate for the audience, the size of the room and your own ability to use it effectively.

* Visual aids contain skeleton information, while handouts are fully fleshed out. They are not interchangeable.

★ Don't subject your audience to masses of figures or complete sentences and paragraphs on the screen. They can concentrate on only one thing at a time, and it won't be you.

★ Illustrate statistics, business trends and other financial information by charts and graphs. If you must use words only, set them out as word charts and don't use complete sentences.

★ The main purpose of handouts is for review after the presentation, so they need to contain complete information. Effective visual aids are not appropriate for this purpose, so don't make them do double duty.

5 Listen to What You Are Hearing

Listening is not the same as hearing, nor is it waiting for your turn to speak.

In this chapter, five things that really matter:
~ Avoid selective listening
~ Listen for the context
~ Separate fact from propaganda
~ Listen for the speaker's feelings and control your own emotions
~ Recognize male/female differences in speaking styles

People often complain that no one ever tells them anything. Rarely, however, do you hear those same people admit that they never listen, which is usually the real problem. Most of us don't listen as well as we think we do, and some don't listen at all.

One reason is confusion between listening and hearing. Hearing involves only the mechanism inside your ears. Sound waves reverberate off your eardrum, producing words you can recognize, as well as other sounds you must interpret. It happens all the time, even with sounds of which you are not consciously aware: traffic in the street, radio or television playing in the background, the conversation at the next table in the restaurant. But that's not listening.

When someone else is speaking, you usually are not, so there will be silence from your side of the conversation. But if you are running over your reply in your mind and just waiting until the other person finishes so that you can jump in, that's not listening. Listening is a conscious act, and if we don't practise it actively and carefully, we simply cannot communicate effectively and fully.

Is this you?

• I have a colleague I don't like, and he never tells me anything. • People are always telling me I've missed the point. • I'm too easily persuaded and I usually don't realize it is happening until it's too late. • When someone makes me mad it's difficult for me to continue the conversation rationally. • Our staff includes men and women, and I sometimes think we are speaking different languages.

Avoid selective listening

Many people hear only what they want to hear. A man is surprised when he is turned down for a job, because the interviewer said he had the right qualifications. He conveniently missed the comment that there were nine other applicants.

In business, we can't afford to practise selective listening. The fact that we ignore the bad news doesn't make it go away. In fact, things might well become worse if we act on just one part of a complex message.

Someone says half a sentence and we immediately leap to the end, assuming we know what they were about to say and so we don't listen to the rest. Not only can we easily 'hear' the wrong information, but we also run the risk of antagonizing the speaker.

A common cause of selective listening is

personal bias against the speaker. It's tempting to discount the opinions of people you simply don't like.*

If you feel yourself mentally switch off when a certain person begins to speak, you are guilty of selective listening. Remember, the information may be valid and useful even if the person delivering it is not on your friendship list.

Listen for the context

A mark of the expert communicator is the ability to hear what is not said. Every comment we make fits into a context, without which it makes no sense or may have a different meaning altogether. If you ask your child to run to the corner store on an errand, for example, and she replies, 'It's raining', you might realize she is offering the weather as a reason not to go. On the other hand, someone looking out of the window on arising in the morning may make the same comment simply as a fact related to nothing

* Don't discount the importance of the message, simply because you don't care for the messenger.

in particular.

The ability to listen for context can stop us from taking the discussion off track.*

Someone speaks up at a meeting, suggesting a promotional event as part of a new product launch. As background he cites a street party that took place in his neighbourhood to raise awareness of traffic safety. One colleague responds by doubting the appropriateness of a street party to this business, while another begins to rail about deteriorating driving habits. The effective listener, however, realizes the context, and responds with a question about the speaker's ideas for a promotional event. Expert listeners recognize the difference between the main point of the statement and the illustrative example.

Separate fact from propaganda

To be an effective listener you must learn to decide what is fact and what is just someone else's opinion or what they would like you to believe. People colour their words in many

* Considering the context is essential to understanding the message.

ways, adding to the challenge of listening.

The bandwagon effect

'Everybody does it.' This is the bandwagon effect. Of course we all recognize this tactic in advertising, but we don't always notice it in normal conversation. Any time someone is trying to persuade you to do something or believe something, listen carefully for the facts and strip away the opinion.

Janice works in a stock-brokerage house. By working hard and learning the business, she has steadily moved up to the top of the 'non-professional' ranks and makes good money. However, her boss is now encouraging her to go one step further by taking the industry examination that would vault her into the 'professional' ranks and open up a whole new world of career possibilities. She is discussing this with her co-worker, Sharon, who has not risen as high or as quickly. Sharon says, 'If I were you I wouldn't bother with the exam. *Everybody* says it's too much work. You have to put your life on hold just to pass the exam. And *nobody* ever really gets promotion because of it anyway. Just stay as you are.' Janice knows a number of people who have successfully taken the exam without giving up their other activities, and several of them have done very well in their careers. So, if she is a lively listener, she can separate what has been said into fact (others have succeeded through taking the exam) and the 'bandwagon' propaganda Sharon is presenting.

Biased talk

Another way facts can be distorted is with biased words and expressions. Politicians are experts at this tactic. If a politician wants to make a straightforward statement about the country, he or she will call it that: the 'country'. If a little more of a statesmanlike feeling is wanted, it might move up a notch to the 'nation', and if they really want to tug at the heartstrings they will talk about 'this land'! Words have their own emotional temperatures, which can subtly alter the message they convey. An active listener recognizes this type of propaganda and can see through it to the message itself.

People sometimes have so much vested interest in their opinions being accepted that they sound like a television evangelist in full swing. 'This new process will revolutionize the way our company operates' they say. That may well be true, but it may not be the kind of revolution you want! Or it may not be true at all. Learn to strip away the opinion and propaganda and listen for the facts before you decide how to respond.*

Listen for the speaker's feelings and control your own emotions

When people are angry, upset or fearful, an effective listener will work to defuse the emotion before dealing with the words. Parents instinctively follow this practice, and business people can learn from them. When a small child falls and scrapes a knee the mother will typically comfort the child with a hug before going on to deal with the wound.

In the same way, irate customers want you to recognize their pain before moving on to

* Ask yourself if the statement is true, or just the speaker's opinion.

discuss possible actions. If you respond by asking for factual information first (such as name, address, credit card number, etc) the customer will stay on the same level of anger, making it difficult to deal with the problem. Often a simple, 'Oh dear, I can understand why that would frustrate you' can go halfway towards correcting the problem.

You must also listen to *yourself*, so that you can recognize and deal with your own emotional responses. We all have 'hot buttons' – attitudes and beliefs that make us respond with a sudden flash of anger when people raise certain topics or express particular opinions. What are *your* hot buttons? It's important to be aware of them so that you can decide how to react, rather than be led by your emotions.

Depending on the subject, the speaker and the purpose of the discussion, you might choose one of three options:

~ Ignore the comment and move on.

~ Make an issue of the remark.

~ Make a passing comment, and then

continue the conversation on the original track.

There are appropriate occasions for each. The important thing is that you should make the choice consciously. When you lose control of your emotions in a business discussion, effective communication is often lost.*

Recognize male/female differences in speaking styles

If you travel in a foreign country you will always be at an advantage if you understand the local language. In the same way, you will understand and work better with people of the opposite sex if you understand the differences in the way we communicate.

The most noticeable difference is this: women like to give and receive details, while men prefer to 'cut to the chase'. This difference gives rise to misunderstanding, because each mistakenly attributes attitudes to the other, based on their own style rather than that of the other.

Let's say, for example, that you are

* Feelings contribute to human interactions as much as words. Effective listeners respond to feelings first, then words.

returning an item to a store for a refund. If the attendant is a woman she will want details of why you are returning the item: is it the wrong colour, a poor fit, damaged. She won't mind if you go into detail about how you decided it was wrong, or that your spouse was the one who was not satisfied with it. A man in the same position, however, will require details only to the extent the store policy calls for them. Otherwise, simply say you are returning the item for a refund.

This might be the reason that women often accuse men of not listening, to which men reply that women never get to the point. In fact it's simply a matter of style. Women tend to discuss details as a way of understanding a situation, while men feel more in control when they reach a conclusion quickly.

Consideration of gender style differences is part of the arsenal of an effective listener.*

* *If the speaker is of the opposite sex, you must adjust your listening filter to accommodate a different style.*

Summary points

★   Listen to what is said, not to what you want to hear. Hear the speaker out to the end, rather than assuming you know what is in his or her mind.

★ A statement out of context can take on a different meaning. So it is important to probe for understanding of context before continuing the discussion.

★ You may be willing to be persuaded by the speaker's argument, but it should be your choice. Learn to separate fact from opinion.

★ Disregarded emotions will escalate, and can turn a discussion into an argument. Acknowledge feelings before responding to the words. Control your own emotions, and consciously choose how you will respond to someone pushing your 'hot button'.

★ Study the communication style of the opposite sex, and use your understanding of the differences to raise the level and clarity of communication.

6 Take an Active Part in the Listening Process

Sometimes the speaker leaves gaps in the information being conveyed. An effective listener knows how to dig for the missing pieces.

In this chapter, four things that really matter:
~ The art of questioning
~ Non-verbal cues
~ Acknowledgement and feedback
~ Reflective listening

In the last section we dealt with how the listener receives information. There is, however, a more active part you can play which, when mastered, can help the process by eliciting the information you want.

It's more difficult to concentrate on listening to a person who is delivering a one-way speech, when you are unable to ask questions or clarify what you hear. Often a speaker needs to be redirected to be understood; to receive indications that you are not only hearing but understanding. Sometimes, in order to receive and understand the speaker's message, you need clarification, and the best way to receive it is to ask for it. That's why listening sometimes involves speaking.

Messages are also sent and received through non-verbal signals such as body language and tone of voice.*

Is this you?

• What do people mean by open and closed questions? I don't understand the purpose.
• I take what people say to be true and am often surprised when I seem to have misunderstood. • I feel I always listen to what people are saying, but they often ask me if I am listening. • My boss's instructions are sometimes vague. How can I make sure I have the right information?

* *Ignore non-verbal signals and you run the risk of receiving the wrong message.*

The art of questioning

The listening process includes helping the

other party to convey his or her thoughts. By asking the right questions you can greatly affect the breadth and depth of the conversation.*

That is the real art of listening. Here's how effective questioning works.

1. **Closed question:** Is communication effective at your company?

2. **Open question:** What communication mechanisms do you have at your company?

The first example is a closed question, which means it can be answered by a simple yes or no. The second is an open question, because the other person must elaborate and give information in order to answer it. Both types of questions have their uses. If you want to develop and broaden a conversation, start by asking open-ended questions. Then, as the need for confirmation arises, insert closed-ended questions where appropriate.

* Questioning is a valid and helpful aspect of listening, so it's important to work on it.

Continuing the example:

Interviewer: What communication mechanisms do you have at your company?

President: We have newsletters, monthly management/staff meetings and our Intranet.

Interviewer: How does this help you get your management message across?

President: We use them for special announcements, etc.

Interviewer: What would be an example of that?

President: Well, last month we announced our new product line in the newsletter, and then used the monthly meeting as an opportunity for staff to ask questions about it. I was very happy with the discussion.

Interviewer: So you think the combination of two vehicles worked well in this instance?

President: Yes.

You can use both types of questions to

broaden a conversation, confirm or clarify meaning and then move the conversation in another direction. Here are examples of how you use questions for these purposes.

Broadening

~ Mary, you've told us about the new procedure they are using in the northern branch and it seems to be working well. How do you think we can adapt it to suit our conditions in the south?

~ We've agreed that we have a major problem competing against the established brand in the marketplace. Does anyone have any ideas as to how we can make people notice our house brand?

Note: These questions call for an analytic response that will bring in more information and broaden the discussion.

Clarifying or confirming

~ What do you mean?

~ Are you saying you agree with Doug's assessment?

~ So, you think we can achieve our sales target for this quarter?

Note: By asking these questions you give the speaker an opportunity to restate a position and clarify it for the other parties.

Changing direction

~ We've discussed your proposed programme in depth and it seems to have merit. What impact will it have on the budget?

~ OK. I see how a marketing blitz would help us raise awareness of the product line. But how can we do this with the small number of sales reps we have?

Note: These questions bring closure to one part of the discussion and move it on to another aspect.

So open-ended questions elicit information and closed-ended ones serve to confirm information or opinion. Think about your own conversations. Do you use questions effectively?*

* *The right questions can help you fill in gaps in the speaker's message*

Non-verbal cues

Suppose for a moment that you live in a different place from the one where you grew up, and you have gone 'home' on vacation. For the first week you have spent every day and evening with your mother, and you have thoroughly enjoyed her company. Now an old friend has invited you out for dinner. As you leave you say, 'OK Mum, I'm off. I'll probably be at Barbara's place for a couple of hours after dinner, so I won't be too late back.' Instead of looking at you with her usual cheerful face, Mum looks down at the carpet, her head leans forward and down to one side and her voice seems to have slowed down and aged 20 years as she says, in a world-weary tone, 'Oh don't worry, I'll be fine. Just you go ahead and enjoy yourself, and don't give a thought to me at all. I'll be fine.'

This is a classic case of the non-verbal cues – body language and tone of voice – being in direct conflict with the spoken words. Mum's non-verbal message is clear: she doesn't want you to go, she would prefer that you didn't enjoy yourself and she is not fine at all!

It's not only in personal situations that this type of conflict arises. People send non-verbal messages in the workplace all the time, and effective listeners have learned to 'hear' them. Note that how you decide to respond is not the issue here – the important thing is that you recognize the underlying message.

There are two types of non-verbal cue: body language and tone of voice.

1. Body language

Although the body often speaks loudly, its language is not an exact one. There is danger in interpreting individual gestures and mannerisms according to a fixed set of 'rules', because they do not always mean the same thing from one person to another. For example, conventional wisdom tells us that folded arms indicate defensiveness or unwillingness to be persuaded; however, many people (including me) fold their arms simply because they find it a comfortable position! Another commonly held belief is that you can't trust someone who doesn't look you in the eye. The problem is, someone who is an accomplished liar probably knows this, and is quite prepared to look you solemnly in the eye and lie quite happily!

Does this mean body language isn't relevant? No, it doesn't. But it has led to the more reliable measure of 'body language clusters'. If your boss stands in front of your desk with arms folded while asking for information, it doesn't necessarily mean anything. But if she folds her arms and at the same time taps her foot, frowns and clenches her teeth – tread warily in your response to the question.

What the good listener looks for is body language that seems to contradict the words the speaker is saying. When they are in direct conflict, usually the body language is a truer indication of meaning.

2. Tone of voice

Have you ever heard a speaker stand up on the platform and begin a speech with the words, 'I'm pleased to be here with you today' – spoken in a flat monotone that indicated no pleasure at all? You probably noticed that the tone of voice didn't match the words – and you believed the tone. Most people would. What did that do for the speaker's credibility? My guess is: not much.

Tone of voice plays a much more important part in our conversations than we realize. On hearing their voices on a tape recording for the first time, most people refuse to believe they sound 'like that'. Often they don't realize that they speak in such a flat tone, but the tape is proof that many of us do.

So how does this information help us listen? It gives us another tool to evaluate the truth and sincerity of the person's actual words and the feelings behind them.

Effective listeners always pay attention to the non-verbal cues because they are a vital component of communication.*

.* For a message to be clear and uncomplicated, the words, body language and tone of voice should all be saying the same thing.

Acknowledgement and feedback

You can acknowledge what someone is saying through a verbal or non-verbal response. A simple nod of the head, a smile, a raising of the eyebrows: these are all forms of non-verbal acknowledgement. They let the speaker know that you are paying attention.

You might inject into the conversation such phrases as: *I understand ... Really? ... I didn't know that*. This indicates your understanding, not necessarily your agreement. If you don't agree, your chance to express your concerns will come later.

These forms of acknowledgement demonstrate your interest and deepen the rapport between you and the speaker.

Acknowledging feelings

In a meaningful conversation, each party acknowledges the other's *feelings* as well as the actual words that are spoken. For example, suppose a co-worker is complaining bitterly to you about a seemingly trivial matter. Joanna frowns and angrily exclaims, 'Why don't they print these meeting announcements on coloured paper or something? How do they expect me to pay attention to yet another piece of white paper that gets lost among everything else on this desk?' You could, of course, simply agree that it's an interesting idea, or you could say you don't have a problem with the white paper – but in either case you might well be missing the point. If, on the other hand, you respond to Joanna's feelings and say, 'This really seems to have you upset,' you open up the possibility for her to explore the reason for this. Before long it becomes apparent that Joanna is feeling overwhelmed by her workload, and the announcement buried on the papers on her desk is just the last straw. Effective listening provides a positive contribution to the discussion.

Different reactions

Men and women react differently to this type of acknowledgement. Often, men are reluctant to discuss their feelings, and are quite likely to deny them. When responding to a man in this situation, make sure you preface with an exploratory phrase such as *it seems to me*, *could it be*, or *I wonder if*. Women tend to be more open to comment on their feelings, although you still need to proceed with some sensitivity.

Showing understanding

Be careful of the language you use in giving feedback. If you use phrases such as *my advice is*, *your problem is* or *what you should do*, you may think this is positive feedback. However, it may not be welcome. If you give the speaker an opportunity to talk the problem through, he or she will often come up with the answer, which is much more effective. Sometimes a well-meaning listener may downplay a problem with a response like *don't worry*, or *that's not so bad*. Again, this may seem like encouragement, but it can actually be perceived as devaluing the person's concern. Sometimes an effective listener needs to offer evidence of understanding, rather than trite assurances.*

Reflective listening

Reflective listening is a form of acknowledgement and feedback that is open to some misunderstanding and misuse. As the name suggests, it simply means taking the message the speaker is sending and returning

* *It's important to the speaker that you not only listen, but be seen to be listening.*

it to the speaker for confirmation. However, reflecting is not the same as parroting! Before sending the message back, you need to rephrase it. Consider, for example: the following:

Richard: I'm fed up writing draft reports for Tom to take to the meetings and then never hearing whether they went anywhere or not.

Jerry: So what you're saying is that you're fed up writing draft reports for Tom to take to the meetings and then never hearing whether they went anywhere or not. Is that right?

That's pretty silly, isn't it? That's parroting. Putting it in the form of reflective listening would result in something like this:

Richard: I'm fed up writing draft reports for Tom to take to the meetings and then never hearing whether they went anywhere or not.

Jerry: It sounds as if you are frustrated by not receiving feedback from Tom about your reports. Is that right?

That's reflective listening. It can be a very useful method of making sure, for example, that you have instructions correct before acting on them.*

Summary points

★ When you need more details than the speaker is giving, ask appropriate questions. Use open-ended questions to broaden the discussion, closed-ended ones for confirmation of facts.

★ Words are just part of the message. Pay attention to body language and tone of voice. If they don't agree, often the non-verbal cues contain the real message.

★ Use gestures and comments to let the speaker know you are listening. This will encourage the flow of information.

★ When clarity is essential and the message is vague, restate it in terms that reflect your understanding. This gives the speaker an opportunity to confirm your understanding or, alternatively, make the point more clearly.

* *When the message is unclear you can help the speaker by 'reflecting' a statement in slightly different terms to clarify it.*